Animal  Lives

DOLPHINS AND PORPOISES

Sally Morgan

QED Publishing

QED

Written by Sally Morgan
Design and editorial by East River Partnership

Publisher Steve Evans
Creative Director Zeta Davies

Printed and bound in China

Picture Credits

Key: t = top, b = bottom, l = left, r = right,
c = centre, FC = front cover

Corbis /Jeffrey L. Rotman 10–11, 30r, /Neil
Rabinowitz 13, /DB Wolfgang Runge/dpa 23;
Ecoscene /Phillip Colla 4–5, 17b; **Getty** /Flip
Nicklin 7, /Kim Westerskov 18, /Norbert Wu
24–25, /Flip Nicklin 25t, /Stephen Frink 28–29,
/Flip Nicklin 28b; **Photolibrary** /Gerard Soury
4m, /David Fleetham 14b, /Pacific Stock/James
Watt 14–15; **Photoshot/NHPA** /Mark Bowler
8–9; **Shutterstock** /Albert Campbell 1t, /Tom
Hirtreiter 1, /Specta background, /Hiroyuki
Saita 5b, /Bryan Michael Dirk 6, /Cindy
Davenport 12, /Mikael Damkier 16–17, /Kristian
Sekulic 19, 20–21, 26, /Wolfgang Amri 20b,
/Karisa Hess 21t, /Jan van der Hoeven 22,
/Peter Asprey 27, /Sergey Popov V 30l,
/Hiroshi Sato 30m.

Words in **bold** are explained
in the Glossary on page 31.

Contents

Dolphins and porpoises

Dolphins and porpoises are intelligent animals that live in the world's seas and rivers. Although they have a fish-like body and flippers, they do not have **gills** like fish. Instead, they have a pair of lungs. This means that, unlike fish, they have to come to the surface of the water to breathe.

Dolphins and porpoises live in groups called pods, which can be very large.

Even large dolphins like to leap out of the water when they swim close to the surface.

Marine mammals

Dolphins and porpoises are **mammals.** This means that the females give birth to live young and feed them milk. Unlike most other mammals, dolphins and porpoises do not have body hair. Their skin is sleek, smooth and rubbery to the touch. They belong to a group of mammals called **cetaceans**, which includes the whales.

Sows, bulls and calves

Dolphins and porpoises live in family groups. The female is called a sow, the male is a bull and the young are called calves.

Dolphins are mammals and have flippers instead of legs.

Dolphin and porpoise types

There are 37 types, or species, of dolphin and six types of porpoise. All porpoises live in the sea, while five species of dolphin live in rivers.

The small spinner dolphin lives mainly in tropical waters.

Dolphin or porpoise?

As dolphins and porpoises look very similar, the best way to tell them apart is to look at their teeth. Dolphins have sharp, cone-shaped teeth, while porpoises have spade-shaped teeth.

River dolphins

River dolphins are small. Some are just one metre long. River dolphins have a long, slender beak and a large, bulging forehead. Their eyes are small and, unlike other dolphins, they have a neck.

Most of the long-beaked river dolphins have poor eyesight.

Finding dolphins and porpoises

Dolphins and porpoises live in all of the world's oceans and seas, even in the very cold waters of the Arctic. Some, such as the common dolphin and bottlenose dolphin, are found all around the world. Others are only found in certain oceans. The Pacific white-sided dolphin, for example, only lives in the Pacific Ocean.

The Amazon River dolphin lives in the Amazon and Orinoco rivers of South America.

Shallow or deep water?

Some dolphins and porpoises, such as harbour porpoises and the vaquita, prefer to stay close to land in shallow water. The vaquita is a type of porpoise that lives in lagoons off the west coast of Mexico. The Risso's dolphin, on the other hand, prefers to live in deeper waters far out to sea.

Saltwater and freshwater

River dolphins are found in many large rivers, including the Amazon in South America, the Indus in Pakistan and the Ganges in India. These dolphins are named after the river in which they live. The Amazon River dolphin, which can survive in saltwater and freshwater, is often seen in the Amazon **estuary**. Here, river freshwater mixes with sea saltwater.

This map shows where dolphins and porpoises are found in the world's oceans and rivers.

Ocean dolphins ■
River dolphins ●

Giving birth

After a bull and sow dolphin have come together to mate, the sow will be **pregnant** for one year. She then gives birth to one calf in the water, which is born tail first. Soon after the birth, the sow pushes her calf to the water's surface so that it can take its first breath.

As dolphins breathe through a **blowhole** on the top of their head, the newborn calf has to learn when to open and close its blowhole to avoid breathing in water!

A newly born bottlenose dolphin calf weighs about 6-8 kilograms and is up to one metre long.

First month

The hungry calf quickly starts feeding on its mother's milk, which is rich in fat and helps the calf to grow quickly. During the first month, the calf stays close to its mother's side. Her movements in the water help to pull the calf gently along.

Dolphin fact!

The Indus River dolphin sometimes carries its young on its back, above the surface of the water.

11

Growing up

The young calf feeds on its mother's milk for about one year after it is born. When it is three months old, however, the calf's first teeth appear and it starts to eat fish as well.

Dolphin fact!

Adult dolphins sometimes show younger dolphins how to put small bits of sponge on their beak for protection while hunting for food on the rough sea floor.

By playing together, young dolphins learn many skills that they will need as adults.

Learning from play

Dolphin calves spend a lot of time playing with their mother and with other calves in the pod. They dart about the waves created by boats and leap out of the surf. Playing is important for young dolphins as it teaches them how to communicate with each other and how to hunt for food.

Dolphins enjoy racing through the water ahead of boats.

Living in pods

Most pods contain about ten dolphins or porpoises, although the biggest pods can have many thousands of animals in them. A typical pod is made up of mothers and their calves together with a few bulls. Sometimes, a pod is formed from dolphins or porpoises that are not related.

Hunting together

When out hunting, a pod communicates by whistling. Sometimes, pods join together to form large hunting herds. If a mother joins a hunting group, her calves are often looked after by other sows in the pod.

The tiger shark is a predator of dolphins and porpoises.

14

This pod of spinner dolphins is made up of sows, calves and a few bulls.

Dolphin fact!

A dolphin's main enemies are sharks and orcas, or killer whales. When under attack, members of a pod work together to chase off a **predator**.

Leaving the pod

A calf is cared for by its mother for the first two years of its life, sometimes even longer. After this, a female calf usually stays in her mother's pod, while a male calf joins another pod.

A life in water

Dolphins and porpoises spend their whole life in water, rising to the surface to breathe. When they surface, they open the blowhole on the top of their head and let out the air in their lungs with a spurt. This blows away water in their blowhole so that when they breathe in again, no water gets into their lungs.

Keeping warm

It is important for dolphins and porpoises to keep their body temperature at 36°C. This is almost the same temperature as a human being. To do this, dolphins and porpoises have a thick layer of fat under their skin that traps heat in their body and keeps them warm in cold ocean waters.

Dolphins come to the surface to breathe every two minutes or so. When necessary, however, they can hold their breath for longer.

A dolphin's blowhole is on the top of its head, behind its bulging forehead.

Dolphin fact!

The deepest dive recorded for a bottlenose dolphin is 300 metres. This was made by a dolphin named Tuffy, who was kept by the United States Navy.

Swimming

The dolphin's torpedo-shaped body is perfect for swimming. Its smooth surface allows it to move easily through the water at high speed. The dolphin uses its powerful tail to push itself forward and its two flippers to steer and brake.

The surface of the skin of a dolphin is hairless and very smooth.

Porpoise fact!

The Dall's porpoise, which can reach speeds of about 55 kilometres an hour, is the world's fastest porpoise.

Spinning through the air

Most dolphins and porpoises enjoy hurling themselves out of the water and leaping in the air. The spinner dolphin, in particular, is a spectacular acrobat that can leap and spin seven times in the air before entering the water again. Some scientists think spinner dolphins do this to shake off fish called remoras, or suckerfish, that stick to their skin.

A spinner dolphin spins its body round as it jumps through the air.

Feeding

Dolphins and porpoises are **carnivores**, or meat eaters. They mainly eat fish, such as anchovies, mackerel, herring and cod, as well as squid.

Swallowed whole

Dolphins and porpoises have small, sharp teeth, which they use to grip a fish's slippery body. As they cannot chew, dolphins and porpoises swallow small fish whole. Before swallowing, however, they carefully position the fish head first to prevent the spines along the back of the fish from sticking in their throat. If a fish is too large to swallow whole, dolphins will rip it up before swallowing it in pieces.

Dolphins eat a wide variety of fish, such as these mackerel.

Dolphins have as many as 90 small, cone-shaped teeth.

Dolphins trap small fish between their teeth and then swallow them whole.

Dolphin fact!

A bottlenose dolphin eats 20 kilograms of fish a day, the weight of 12 chickens.

Senses

Dolphins and porpoises use their senses to find their way around and catch their **prey**. They do not have a sense of smell, but their ears, which are inside their **skulls**, give dolphins and porpoises excellent hearing. Most dolphins and porpoises also have good eyesight, apart from the river dolphins. The Ganges River dolphin is blind.

Dolphin fact!

When dolphins open their eyes underwater, special greasy tears protect them from the stinging salt in seawater.

Echolocation

Dolphins and porpoises can 'see' in water using sound. This is called **echolocation** and is similar to **sonar** used by submarines.

Whistles and clicks

The dolphin uses its **melon** to produce lots of whistles and clicks. These sounds pass through the water and bounce off things to make the echoes that the dolphin uses for echolocation. By listening to these echoes, a dolphin can work out exactly where things are.

The melon is found in the bulging forehead of dolphins and porpoises.

Hunting

Dolphins and porpoises use echolocation to find their fish prey. When the members of a pod come across a **shoal** of fish, they surround it so that the shoal cannot escape. Then one or two members of the pod start to swim through the middle to catch fish.

This dolphin is splitting a shoal of fish by swimming through the middle.

Helping the fishermen

Sometimes dolphins chase fish into shallow water where they are easier to catch. In a town in Brazil, dolphins help the fishermen to catch fish. The fishermen stand on the beach with their nets in the shallow waters while the dolphins drive fish into their nets. The fishermen make sure the dolphins get some of the fish.

Bottlenose dolphins sometimes chase and catch fish in shallow waters.

Dolphin fact!

The Ganges River dolphin swims on its side and drags a flipper along the seabed to find any small animals hiding in the mud.

Communication

Dolphins and porpoises make many sounds to communicate, including squeaks, grunts, trills and even moans. These sounds travel quickly through water, sometimes over long distances. Scientists believe each dolphin has its own type of whistle sound, and that many dolphins can recognize each other by the sound they make.

Dolphins are very talkative and call to each other all the time.

Slapping the water

Dolphins and porpoises also communicate by touching and head-butting each other, or by leaping out of the water. After leaping, they may slap the surface of the water with their tail to make a noise that other dolphins or porpoises will hear.

Dolphins make a lot of noise when they crash down on to the water's surface.

Dolphin fact!

When a calf is born, its mother whistles to it many times. She does this so that her calf learns to recognize her whistle and will always be able to find her, even among lots of other dolphins.

Under threat

Dolphins and porpoises, especially river dolphins, are under threat all around the world. Each year, thousands are killed by hunters or die in fishing nets. Some dolphins even die from lack of food because people have taken too many fish from the waters where they feed. Pollution from chemicals and sewage also harms many dolphins and porpoises.

This rare vaquita porpoise was caught up in a fisherman's net and drowned.

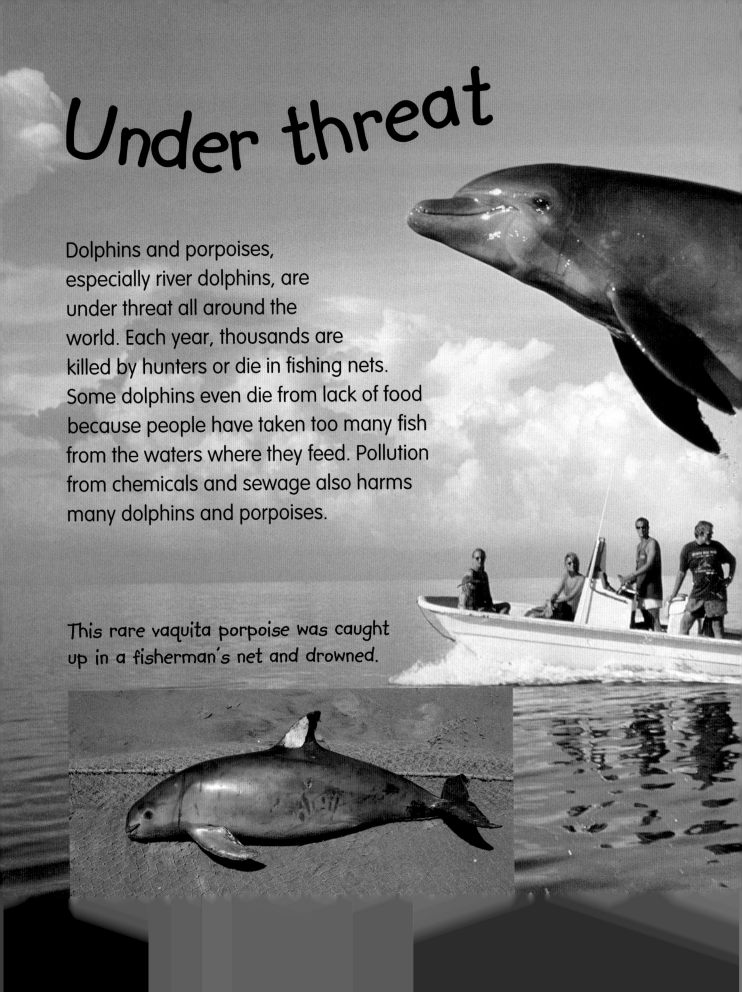

Helping dolphins and porpoises

There are many organizations, such as the Whale and Dolphin Conservation Society, which are working to safeguard dolphins and porpoises. More and more marine nature reserves now also exist where dolphins and porpoises are protected from hunting and fishing. Many fishermen are now helping by using special nets and fishing lines that do not trap dolphins and porpoises.

Dolphin-watching trips are now popular with tourists in many parts of the world.

Porpoise fact!

The rarest porpoise is the vaquita, of which there are only 200 still alive. These are found in the Gulf of California.

Life cycle of a dolphin

A female dolphin is ready to breed when she is four to eight years of age. She is pregnant for one year and gives birth to a single calf. She may have a calf every two to four years. The smaller dolphins and porpoises do not live as long as the larger ones. For example, the small harbour porpoise lives for about 15 years, while the bigger bottlenose dolphin can live for 25 years.

Young calf

Older calf with adult

Adult

Glossary

blowhole the hole in the top of the head of a dolphin, porpoise or whale that is used for breathing

carnivore an animal that eats meat

cetacean a group of marine mammals that includes whales, dolphins and porpoises

echolocation a special ability to 'see' using sound

estuary the mouth of a river

gills organs inside the body of a fish used for breathing in water

mammal an animal that gives birth to live young, rather than laying eggs. Female mammals produce milk to feed their young

melon a structure in the forehead of a dolphin or porpoise used for echolocation

predator an animal that hunts other animals

pregnant a female animal that has a baby, or babies, developing inside her

prey an animal that is hunted by other animals

shoal a group of fish

skull bones in the head that protect the brain

sonar a device used by submarines and ships to find objects in water and calculate how far away they are

Index